Learn about Smart Working

Mike G. Cartright

DEDICATION

I thank all those who contributed to making this text and in particular my wife Mara, my children (Cinzia and Adriano) and my friend Simon

INTRODUCTION

Many companies have increasingly asked their employees to limit their business trips and work in Smart Working, using the available collaboration tools. Today, various governments have launched new policies to contain and manage the epidemiological emergency and are favoring companies to adopt forms of Smart Working. In this scenario, numerous companies have put in place solutions and services to help car washers recover the damage they suffered in terms of health and economically. The Smart Working experienced at this particular moment is a new opportunity to improve with intelligence, new ways of working, new tools, and digital channels. This ebook intends to be a brief reflection on the potential and dangers that smart working poses as a remote working tool. A possible "digital solidarity" to quickly support workers in the correct adoption and correct adoption of intelligent work from a judicial, organizational, and technological perspective. A valid ad hoc training tool to help people improve their ways of working remotely. Understanding this text will allow you to verify the processes, improve the way you work remotely, and improve the interaction between people.

LEARN ABOUT SMART WORKING

Do you know what works intelligently? Well, we've learned it so far. You don't know it yet? Don't worry (for now). This is a new expression of linguistics - around 40% of Spaniards have never heard of it, but that does not mean that you should be satisfied with your ignorance. Do we have more attention? Excellent, he deserves intelligent work, he wants to be recognized worldwide and enjoy a good reputation. Wise work is a new work model that uses new technologies and the development of existing technologies to improve performance and satisfaction gained from work. This should not be confused with the term collaboration, which refers to a common workplace, usually by independent professionals.

Although this is a broad concept, it will have two main ideas: a more cost-effective way to work in many ways, not just in terms of money, and to use technology to get there. The importance of smart work means what it looks like exactly. Yes, so far, everything is "smart" (phone, watch, car ...) and closely linked to the concept of telework. We could also say that intelligent work is a natural progression of the later. It has given the functions of the "traditional" remote control, such as time flexibility or comfort, greater mobility, and well-being. The use of teleworking to move work from the office to the home brings smart work to almost any other location, from a park or cafe to an airport waiting room. Working wisely has advantages and disadvantages for employees—you will find a case study of employees of the business below. However, if you want to know all the pros and cons in more detail, you can access this link https://www.thebalancecareers.com/reasons-why-teleworking-belongs-in-your-future-1919421

It increases the freedom and autonomy of workers. He has a greater ability to organize your time. You can save money on workplaces, transportation, or supplies (electricity, heating, etc.). You can save a lot of time when traveling, especially in big cities. It improves the compatibility of professional and family life, which is often appreciated.

If the work is well organized (usually based on goals), productivity can increase. If an improvement in workers' quality of life is observed, the worker values work and the company. It can attract talent for the business. It allows the integration of people with reduced mobility. The worker sees his personal life as affected by work. This can lead to the separation of the worker because he has no contact with his peers. It can also prevent you from feeling identified with the business. If distance to distance is not properly planned or executed, it can reduce productivity. There may be little control over the quantity or quality of the work. Part of the savings made for the company can mean employee expenses (at the workplace, delivery costs, etc.).

For example, it seems that smart work is widely accepted by those who are more or less clear about what it is. Despite gaps such as disruption and possible divorces, only 17% of job seekers are rejected because of the flexibility offered by judicious work. The study provides other data of interest; For example, it shows the opinion of professionals working in the human resources department. It would be useful for recruits to consider some of the disadvantages of smart jobs, such as B. Separation, less contact with colleagues, or lack of corporate identity. It is useful to combine smart work solutions in the work environment and not at home to combat them. Other interesting facts; 55% of respondents worked at home at some point, and 46.5% would do it from their smartphone. However, one fact is essential: 90.8% of respondents who want to work outside the United States office demonstrate that the old theory of remote working is a passion for many people. Among the privileged rooms, the first came from the house (64.2%), followed by the workrooms (47.6%) or from a place close to the house (41.3%). So it seems more people want to apply smart work to their professional lives than people who know what the term means (don't worry, sometimes these things happen).

As we saw at the beginning of this article, new technologies and improvements to existing technologies are key factors in smart work development. It includes various tools such as the internet, smartphones, social networks, or programs of any kind intended to allow flexibility and job mobility. Not too far in the future, other technologies such as virtual reality are included in the list of technologies that contribute to the development of intelligent work. Some say we have hired our workers in the big cities too long to build our base in regional centers outside of expensive real estate. Others believe that performing skeleton work and unnecessary outsourcing things is the smart way of doing things. Shouldn't you be focus on business results instead of focusing on working in a cafe or reducing your real estate portfolio? It happens in the brain, not in the office.

Optimizing your time is a smart task, but the departure for commuting is not too far away. How many projects are running where many analysts have looked at the data during the month? And what about organizations that don't have Business Intelligence analysts and don't trust competent people to know the next steps and solutions? There is certainly a smarter way to get things done; crowdsourcing, and it works. The OAQ's Fall 2018 edition contains many examples of smart people working on crowdsourcing solutions to meet challenges. We're talking about how Boston's city combined a health inspection prediction algorithm that captures the same number of health violations with 40 fewer notices. Likewise, the Forrester study for Topcoder looked at the savings when an organization uses crowdsourcing and found that the average project duration was reduced by ⅔ and that organizations had access to it three times more with more problem-solving skills. This is better time management and better results, thanks to crowdsourcing. Optimize your time and spend it wisely while transferring difficult jobs to the university audience. The Mathesia platform connects companies with academics who use their specialist knowledge to solve challenges and create value. We call them heads because they are really intelligent and want to deal with soft subjects that would otherwise have their heads down for months or even years. The best scientists and mathematics in the world should work in your business. The challenges are the real "smart" tasks! Mathesia combines people, facts, knowledge, and information to move the business forward. Register here and launch your first challenge or contact us to find out more.

Working wisely involves compromise. On one hand, advantages can result from the flexibility of workplaces and timetables: employees reduce their travel costs, and companies increase their costs (lighting, heating or air conditioning, canteens, cleaning, etc.). By leaving the defined daily start and end, employees can better manage their time according to their needs. For personal or family reasons, they can take long or short breaks and adapt their working hours to changing living conditions without changing their wages. It increases their pleasure and their work-life balance, which ultimately makes these regulations favorable to employees. At the same time, companies can optimize by rewarding these employees for efficient productivity rather than for a few hours of work. Businesses can also benefit from a talent retention and reduced absence days, thereby increasing their competitiveness. In addition, the flexibility of the labor market for all workers (men and women) helps to reduce rewards in long-term, specific and flexible hours, which is believed to be the main cause of gender wage cuts (Bertrand 2018). This flexibility can be a step towards the "last chapter of the great success of the sexes" (Goldin 2014). On the other hand, smart work raises many concerns. Working outside the workplace can reduce employee engagement, reduction in interactions between workers and supervisors tends to reduce productivity, especially in high-engagement jobs. After all, blurring the lines between work and home, and employee stress can increase over time and make balancing work-life more difficult.

In a recent article (Angelici and Profeta 2020), we empirically study how smart workers are introduced into this approach. We are designing a randomized experiment to study the causal effects of the introduction of smart work with a large traditional company in the multi-service sector in Italy. The company has never worked flexibly before. Using the Randomized Control Study (RCT) method, we selected a sample of 310 workers (which included employees and workers) and randomized them into two groups: workers in the first group (group treatment) have the possibility of nine months, working "wisely" for a long time, one day in a week in consultation with their superiors (that is to say without any restriction as to the place or time). Workers in the second group (the control group) continued to work traditionally. We are interested in three key results in three dimensions: productivity, well-being, and work-life balance. We use objective measures of employee performance calculated monthly by the company (for example, the number of files processed during the month) and the number of vacation days that each employee takes. We supplement this information with questions asked from each employee and their supervisors before and after treatment. The questions cover different dimensions of self-productivity, well-being, work and family compatibility. Given the randomization of the two groups, we can identify the causal effect of the treatment's causal effect on our outcomes of interest. Our results show that workers wisely increase their productivity in the same period of time compared to workers who continued to work traditionally. This result applies regardless of whether productivity is measured by an objective measure or measured using certain specific productivity characteristics (for example, timeliness) declared by the employee or by the manager himself.

Sex also has interesting effects. First, men spend more time on household chores and repairs. This means that, smart work, although not a gender policy, helps to improve the gender balance in the family, which is an important step towards gender equality. Second, some results are stronger for women: the reduction of vacations is determined by women, such as the increased enjoyment of smart workers during their working hours. Our results suggest that promoting smart work is an effective way to increase productivity and improve well-being and work-life balance. We also provide evidence that smart work can help reduce gender gaps in the labor market by removing the rigidity associated with certain hours of work (Goldin 2014). Our study, based on intelligent work one day a week, cannot be generalized to the current situation under the coronavirus pandemic, where workers are forced to work from home daily for an extended period. It is interesting to note that the massive unplanned full-time use of smart work shows that it is possible for both professional and non-professional tasks and can be useful in an emergency. However, this will probably have consequences different from those of our study, particularly regarding the workers' feelings of isolation and productivity. However, we suggest that in normal times (for example, after the crisis), the use of smart work can be beneficial for a limited period of the work week.

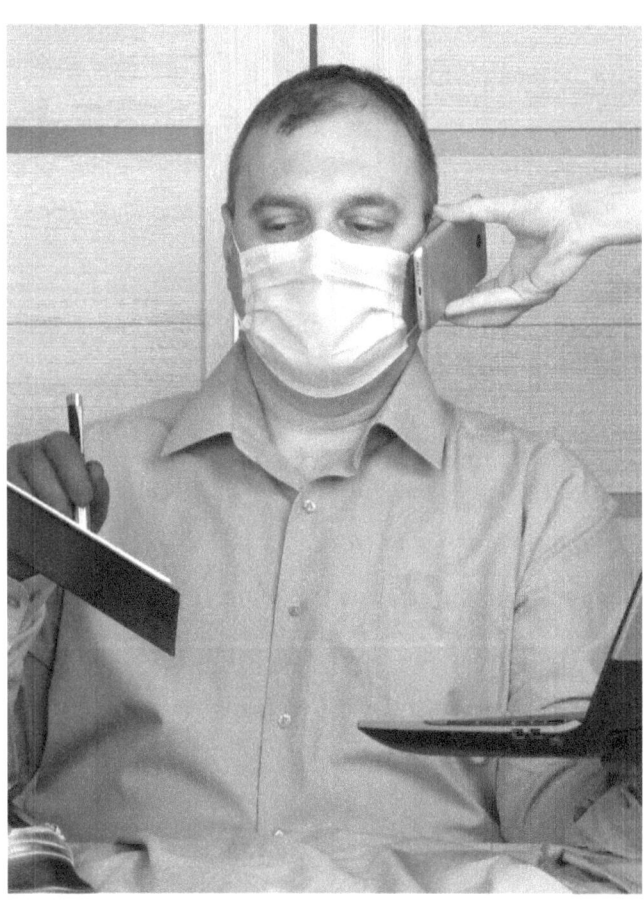

The new millennium and the explosion of Web 2.0 have posed new challenges for businesses. It also means making the work of employees and managers more flexible and "smart" by taking advantage of technological possibilities. If home work was the keyword in the past, we are now talking about a larger and more complex concept beyond "working distance": we are talking about smart work. What is smart work, and how is it done? As already mentioned, smart work is a complex concept because it does not only work remotely in a broader sense. This could include cooperation that is, sharing "open" workplaces with other specialists - mobile work (think about the spread of smartphones and tablets) and 2.0 consulting on the Internet. Employees or consultants working for a company in Smart mode don't have to go to the office every day to do the work. Still, they can do it via an internet connection, a PC, a tablet, and one of the many videos, messaging, or online-Meeting applications (e.g. Skype) communicate securely with their employers or clients).

Therefore, working wisely is a flexible way of working, free from the old business logic, rigid hours, and compulsory presence at the office. Rather, it is a way of presenting result-oriented work. The job market currently requires flexibility: having general skills and problem-solving skills can make a difference. Intelligent work has been established abroad, and it's also developing in Italy: according to the Intelligent Work Observatory of the Polytechnic of Milan, up to 48% of large Italian companies say they are experimenting with this new technique.

January, 2020. The Council of Ministers adopted a law on free and intelligent work (called in the text "agile work"). The law defines smart employment as "a flexible way of working through labor relations to increase productivity to make life and work easier to integrate "; In addition, it defines precise limits, due to the term "agile work" which refers to activities that can be performed both in the office and outside the office but respect the hours of work specified in their contract. Salaries must correspond to employees of the company, such as tax incentives. The employment contract must be written. Obviously, the employer cannot neglect the worker's safety, who must be protected against accidents and be aware of the risks associated with the work to be performed, or his private life. On the other hand, the employee is responsible for the work equipment provided by the company.

Benefits of smart employment in 2014, the Milan Polytechnic Smart Working Observatory calculated that "agile work" could increase business productivity by 27 billion euros and reduce costs by 9 billion euros. Beyond economic data and statistics, work stress is intelligent (because you don't have to travel to get to the company), reduces absenteeism, and increases productivity and flexibility. For a company, this means working remotely with the right employees. The web has removed all barriers. For example, a company based in northern Italy may find the professional they are looking for in Sicily. Agile work expands opportunities, lowers business costs, and even reduces environmental impact.

SMART is a mnemonic/abbreviation that contains criteria for setting goals, e.g. B. for project management, employee performance management, and personal development. The letters S and M generally mean Specific and Measurable. The most common version may contain other letters that indicate Scope, Relevance, and Time. However, the term inventor has a slightly different version, and the letters have different meanings for different authors, as described below. Some authors have added additional letters. The first known use of the term was found in the November 1981 edition of the management review of George T. Doran. The main advantage of SMART goals is that they are easier to understand and to achieve. SMART standards are often associated with the management of Peter Drucker according to the target concept. The word S.M.A.R.T. Objectives and S.M.A.R.T. Objectives appear. Although the acronym SMART generally remains the same, the goals and objectives may differ. Objectives are the clear goals that can be expected from a task or project. On the other hand, the objectives are the defined stages that control the complete achievement of the project objectives. Intelligent systems include acquisition, action and control functions to describe and analyze a situation, make decisions based on available data in a predictive or appropriate manner, and perform judicious actions. In most cases, the "intelligence" of the system can be attributed to an autonomous operation based on regulation, energy efficiency, and network capacities.

Smart work is part of telework, also known as telework. Telework, home work (WFH - the most commonly used term in the UK), mobile work, and flexibility. These are work agreement in which employees do not travel (for example by bus, bicycle or car, etc.) to a central workplace such as an office building, warehouse, or store. Telework was introduced in the 1970s to illustrate telecommunications-related replacements and information technology for travel. 21st century teleworkers often use mobile telecommunications technologies such as a laptop or tablet with Wi-Fi or smartphones to work in cafes; others may use a desktop computer and a home phone. According to a Reuters survey, almost one in five workers worldwide, particularly in the Middle East, Latin America and Asia, often works and accounts for around 10% of their homework daily. In the 2000s, during several years of annual vacation or vacation, organizations were seen as being unemployed rather than resigning, and some office workers used telework to continue reading vacation emails.

In the 1990s, telework became the focus of pop culture's attention. In 1995, the motto was reaffirmed that "work is something you do, not something you travel." Variations of this saying include: "Work is something we do, not a place we go to, and" Work is what we do, not where we are. Telework has been adopted by several businesses, governments, and non-profit organizations. Businesses can use telework to cut costs (teleworkers don't need an office or cubicle, no space to rent or buy, and additional costs such as lighting, air conditioning, etc.). Some organizations use telework to improve the quality of life for workers, as telework generally slows travel and traffic. At the same time, telework makes it easier for workers to reconcile their professional responsibilities with their personal and family responsibilities (for example, childcare or care for older parents). Some organizations use telework for environmental reasons, as telework can reduce congestion and air pollution if fewer cars are driven on the streets.

The roots of telework lay in technology in the early 1970s, connecting satellite offices to telephone lines in the city center via some terminals and telephone lines used as network bridges. The continuous and increasing reduction of costs, as well as the increase in performance and user-friendliness of PCs paved the way for the office to be moved. In the early 1980s, branches and home workers were connected to organizational resources using PCs and terminal emulation. Phone manufacturing is made easier by tools such as groupware, Virtual Private Networks (VPN), conference calls, video conferencing, virtual call centers, Voice Over IP (VOIP) and lower costs for laptop computers with quality. This can be very effective and useful for businesses as it allows employees to communicate over long distances, thus saving a lot of time and travel costs. With the proliferation of broadband Internet connections, more home workers have a large bandwidth to use their tools to connect their home to the intranet and internal company telephone networks. The introduction of Local Area Networks (LAN) has encouraged resource sharing and the client-server computing model for greater decentralization. Now, teleworkers can take laptops with them that they can use in the office, at home, and virtually anywhere. The rise of cloud computing technology and the availability of Wi-Fi have made it possible to access remote servers through a combination of portable hardware and software. In addition, smartphones are used more because of their technological improvements and the growing popularity of telework: worker mobility and an increase.

The available technology is not advanced enough to reproduce personal office interactions. The possibility of errors and misunderstandings may increase. According to the media, richness theory for smart working personal contacts offers the possibility of dealing with detailed information: clear problems can be clarified, immediate feedback can be provided, and personalized communication (e.g. body language, tone of speech: voice).

Different types of communication media should be used for teleworking, e.g. Telephone and email. Emails have a delay that does not allow an immediate return. Phone calls make it difficult to decode the emotions of the person or team on the phone, and these two forms of communication do not allow you to see other people. The organization's standard communication models have been changed in telework. For example, teams that use computer-aided communication at computer conferences make group decisions longer than personal groups. Employees generally enjoy personal contact, phone calls, and one-on-one meetings. Email and the Internet do not contribute to their enjoyment of communication. This suggests that telework may not have the ingredients for "full communication" versus personal interactions. However, research has found that virtual employees on a team are more satisfied with their integrated communication, the same technology as their personal communication in the office.

CONCLUSION

Just as a society, smart working places more emphasis on paid work than unpaid care; there is a social stigma associated with those who work flexibly, especially if they are women.

Mothers can be considered less important employees if they are considered less ambitious or dedicated to their work. This social stereotype may explain the identity gap that people face in wanting to work flexibly and the ramifications they have for slower growth and decline (getting jobs below the previous skill level). In addition, there is a lack of infrastructure for working supervisors, especially inexpensive child care. Sectors are dominated by males and the associated expectation that employees will be the primary supervisors or not. Pioneer organizers of flexible work should also deal with customers who do not. However, the dial changes in society because individual requirements change. The need for flexibility begins with each employee. How comfortable you feel when you work flexibly depends on whether you have managers or an organization willing to accept them. The societal assumption that flexibility only works with mothers and corresponds to someone of professional development is a major challenge.

The following process modifications may be useful: simplify the process of obtaining a flexible employment contract by making it as simple as possible in short, clear forms, with no restrictions as to when individuals can apply, and ensure that the process is clearly signed for employees. Ensure that the HR department is automatically involved in the flexibility requirements to ensure the organization's responsibility and the manager. Create an organization within the organization responsible for overseeing the distribution of flexible work agreements throughout the industry. Behavioral solutions can help managers implement flexible workflows.

Managers and colleagues are essential to the success of flexible on-site work. When superiors have a solid relationship with their employees based on trust, employees can work independently and have control over their working methods. Such management requires solid employee skills but also organizational support. Possible solutions include: helping managers assess and reflect on how flexibility can work for the roles and teams they manage, and publish other successful examples of flexible skills in working in the organization to formal and informal forms. Conduct test periods during which employees test their flexible work agreement so that employees and managers have time to adapt and fit into the agreement or test the whole team's times to be tested. New informal forms of flexible work. Managers in charge of scaling loads in adjusting task flexibility. Make sure objectives are measured so that managers can assess employee performance. Encourage managers to engage in open conversations with their employees about their work-life balance and preferred work styles, and allow managers to prioritize the well-being of 45 employees. Use timely choices, e.g. when employees leave the parent and the discussions that led to it.

REFERENCES

*Angelici, M and P Profeta (2020), "Smart-working: Work flexibility without constraints", Dondena Working Paper 137.

*Bertrand, M (2018), "Coase lecture: the glass ceiling", Economica 85(338): 205–231.

*Bloom, N, J Liang, J Roberts and Z J Ying (2014), "Does working from home work? Evidence from a Chinese experiment", The Quarterly Journal of Economics 130(1): 165–218.

*Eurofound (2017), Working anytime, anywhere: The effects on the world of work.

*Goldin, C (2014), "A grand gender convergence: Its last chapter", American Economic Review 104(4): 1091–1119.Gallup (2017), "State of the American workplace".

*Akhras, G., "Smart Materials and Smart Systems for the Future", Canadian Military Journal, 08/2000European Commission ICT Work Programme 2007-08.

*Callister, P. (2002) "Aging population and social policy in New Zealand: Could family-friendly policies increase both fertility and women's employment?" New Zealand Population Review, 28(2):221-251.

*Department of Labour (2006a) Quality Flexible Work: Increasing

Availability and Take-up in New Zealand, Department of Labour, Wellington.

*Department of Labour (2006b) Work-Life Balance in New Zealand: A Snapshot of Employee and Employer Attitudes and Experiences, Department of Labour, Wellington.

LEARN ABOUT SMART WORKING

The objective of this text is to launch a "Digital Solidarity" intiative, to rapidly support workers in the correct adoption of smart working, from a judicial, organizational and technological point view, with ad hoc training text to help people to improve ways of working remotely. Understanding this text will allow you to verify the processes, improve how to work remotely and improve the interaction between people

Mike G. Cartright ©2020